AF216578

Impressum
Verlag: BABADADA GmbH, Nedderfeld 112 , 22529 Hamburg
Geschäftsführer / Verlagsleitung: Harald Hof
Druck: Books on Demand GmbH, In de Tarpen 42, 22848 Norderstedt

Imprint
Publisher: BABADADA GmbH, Nedderfeld 112 , 22529 Hamburg, Germany
Managing Director / Publishing direction: Harald Hof
Print: Books on Demand GmbH, In de Tarpen 42, 22848 Norderstedt

school
学校

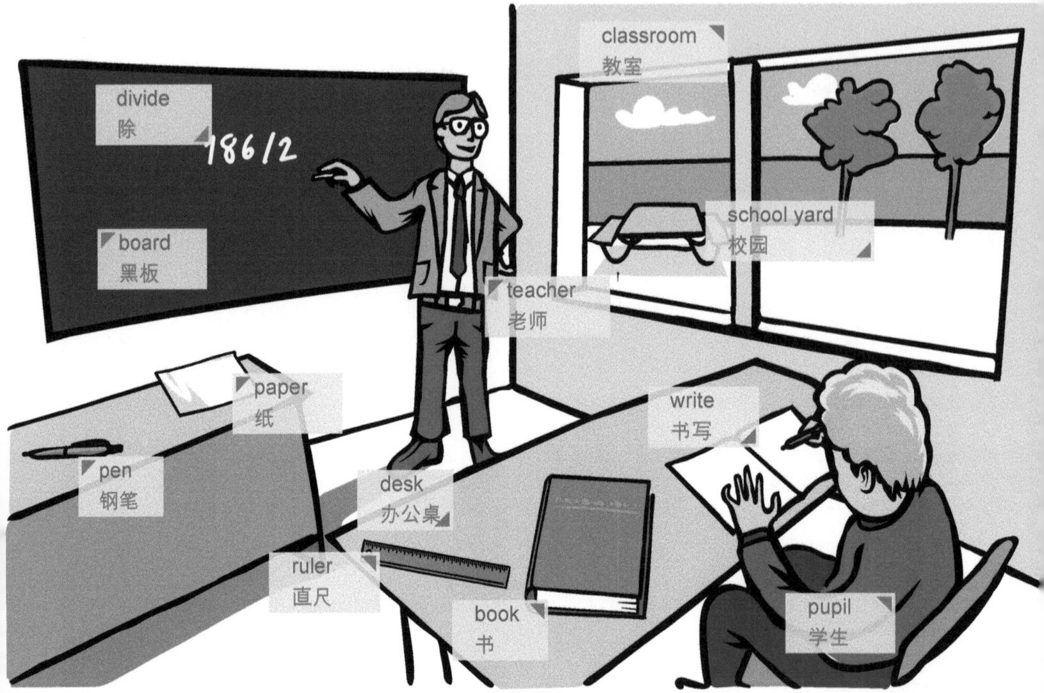
classroom
教室
divide
除
186/2
board
黑板
school yard
校园
teacher
老师
paper
纸
write
书写
pen
钢笔
desk
办公桌
ruler
直尺
book
书
pupil
学生

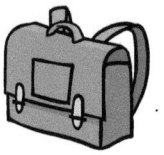

satchel
书包

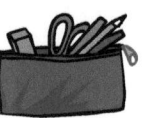

pencil case
铅笔盒

pencil
铅笔

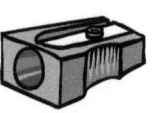

pencil sharpener
卷笔刀

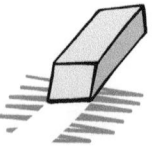

rubber
橡皮擦

drawing pad
画板

drawing

图画

paintbrush

画笔

paint box

颜料盒

scissors

剪刀

glue

胶水

exercise book

练习册

homework

家庭作业

number

数字

add

加

subtract

减

multiply

乘

calculate

计算

letter

字母

alphabet

字母表

word

字

text

课文

read

读

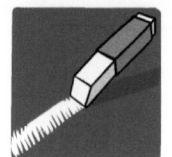

chalk

粉笔

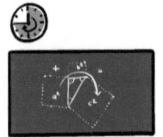

lesson

上课

register

登记

examination

考试

certificate

证书

school uniform

校服

education

教育

encyclopedia

百科全书

university

大学

microscope

显微镜

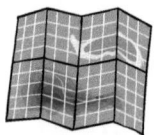

map

地图

waste-paper basket

废纸筐

travel
旅行

hotel
酒店
Grand
hostel
青年旅社
ROOMS
EXCHANGE
currency exchange office
外币兑换处
car
汽车

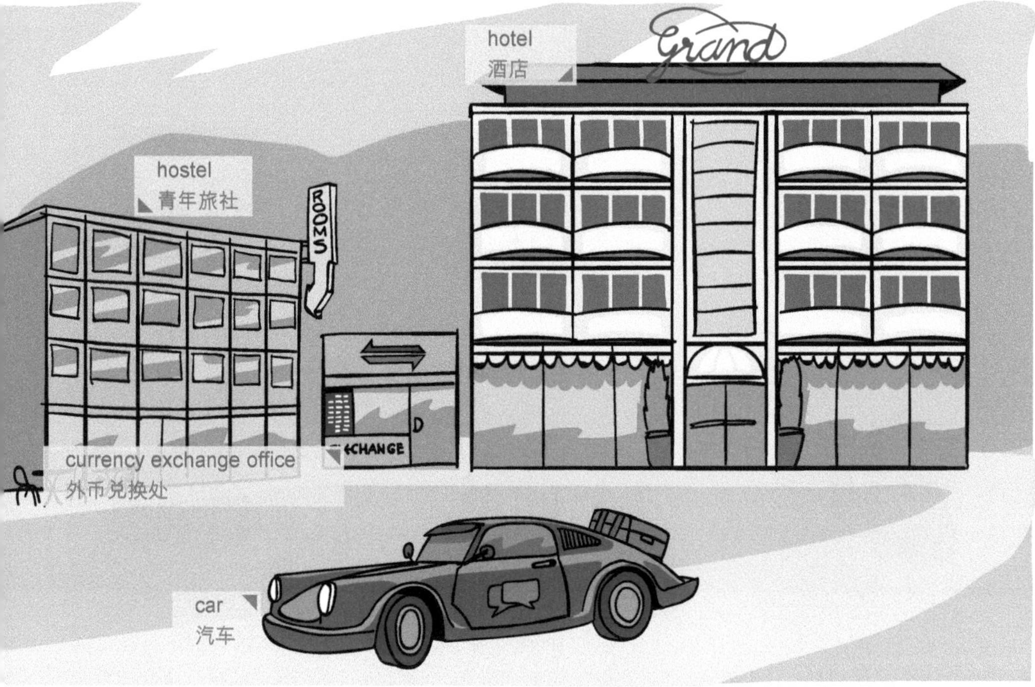

language

语言

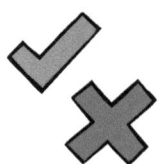

yes / no

是/否

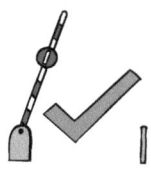

Okay

好的

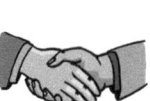

hello

您好

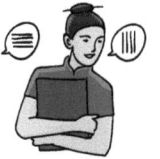

translator

翻译员

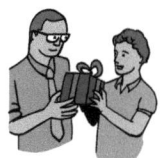

Thank you

谢谢

how much is...?

......多少钱？

I don´t get it

我不明白

problem

问题

Good evening!

晚上好！

Good morning!

早上好！

Good night!

晚安！

goodbye

再见

direction

方向

luggage

行李

bag

包

backpack

双肩包

guest

客人

room

房间

sleeping bag

睡袋

tent

帐篷

tourist information

旅游信息

beach

海滩

credit card

信用卡

breakfast

早餐

lunch

午餐

dinner

晚餐

Ticket

票

elevator

电梯

stamp

邮票

border

边界

customs

海关

embassy

大使馆

visa

签证

passport

护照

transport
交通运输

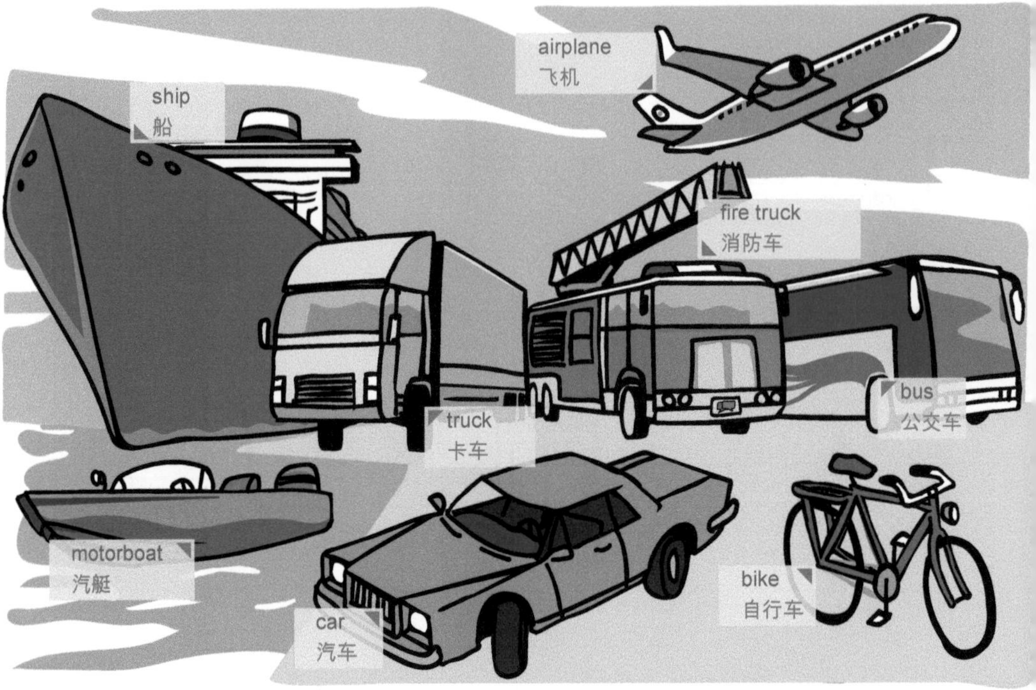
airplane
飞机
ship
船
fire truck
消防车
bus
公交车
truck
卡车
motorboat
汽艇
bike
自行车
car
汽车

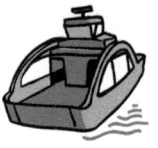

ferry
摆渡船

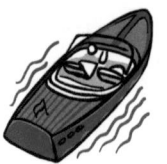

boat
小船

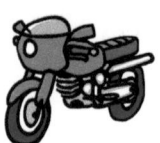

motorbike
摩托车

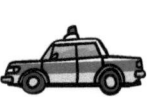

police car
警车

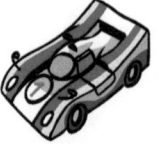

racing car
赛车

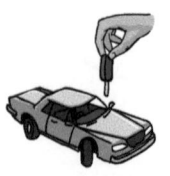

rental car
租车

car sharing

拼车

tow truck

拖车

garbage truck

垃圾车

engine

发动机

fuel

汽油

fuel station

加油站

traffic sign

交通标志

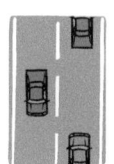

traffic

交通

traffic jam

交通堵塞

parking lot

停车场

train station

火车站

tracks

轨道

train

火车

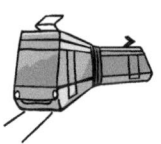

tram

电车

wagon

货车

helicopter

直升机

airport

机场

tower

塔

passenger

乘客

container

集装箱

carton

纸板箱

cart

手推车

basket

篮子

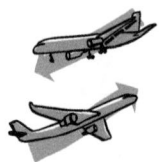

take off / land

起飞/降落

city

城市

village

村庄

city center

市中心

house

房子

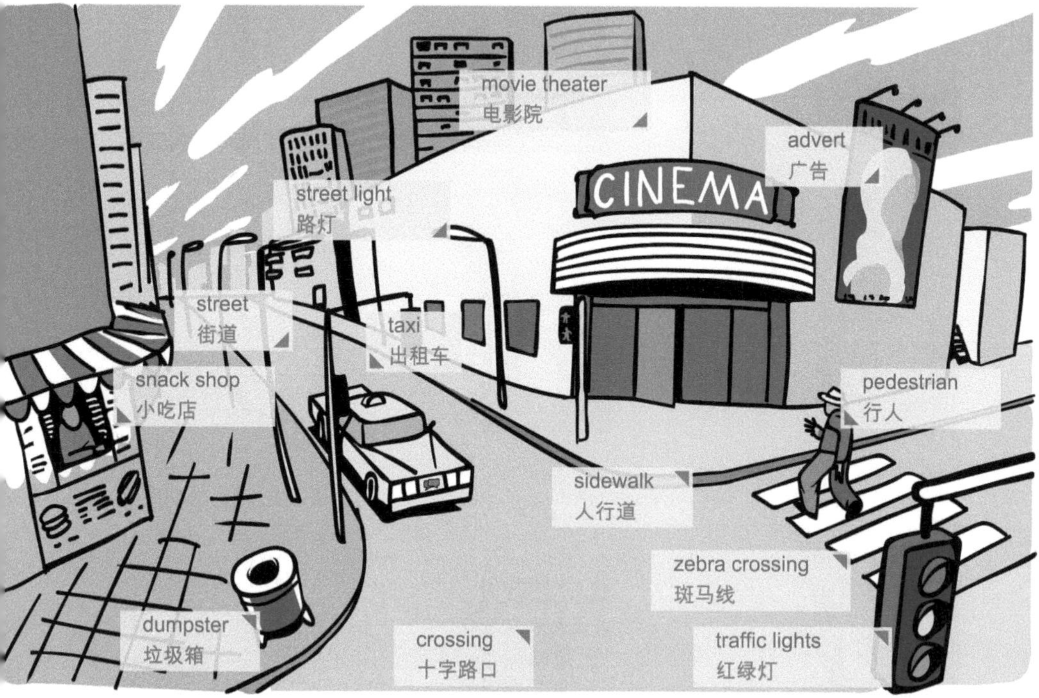

movie theater
电影院
CINEMA
advert
广告
street light
路灯
street
街道
taxi
出租车
snack shop
小吃店
pedestrian
行人
sidewalk
人行道
zebra crossing
斑马线
dumpster
垃圾箱
crossing
十字路口
traffic lights
红绿灯

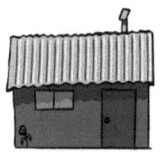

hut

小屋

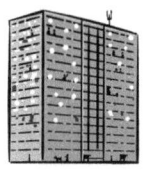

apartment

公寓

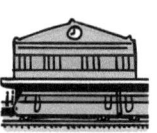

train station

火车站

city hall

市政厅

MUSEUM

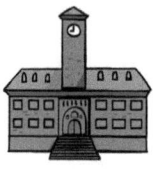

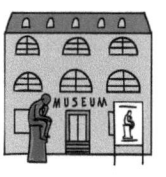

museum

博物馆

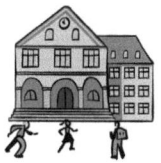

school

学校

university

大学

bank

银行

hospital

医院

hotel

酒店

pharmacy

药房

office

办公室

book shop

书店

shop

商店

flower shop

花店

supermarket

超市

market

市场

department store

百货商店

fishmonger's shop

鱼店

mall

购物中心

harbor

海港

park

公园

bench

长凳

bridge

桥

stairs

楼梯

subway

地铁

tunnel

隧道

bus stop

公交车站

bar

酒吧

restaurant

餐馆

postbox

邮筒

street sign

路标

parking meter

停车计时器

zoo

动物园

swimming pool

游泳馆

mosque

清真寺

farm

农场

pollution

污染

cemetery

墓地

church

教堂

playground

操场

temple

寺庙

landscape

地形

signpost
指示牌

path
路

meadow
草地

stone
石头

tree
树

hiker
徒步旅行者

river
河

grass
草

flower
花

valley

峡谷

hill

山

lake

湖

forest

森林

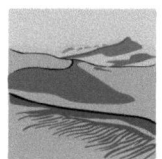

desert

沙漠

volcano

火山

castle

城堡

rainbow

彩虹

mushroom

蘑菇

palm tree

棕榈树

mosquito

蚊子

fly

苍蝇

ant

蚂蚁

bee

蜜蜂

spider

蜘蛛

beetle

甲虫

frog

青蛙

squirrel

松鼠

hedgehog

刺猬

hare

野兔

owl

猫头鹰

bird

鸟

swan

天鹅

boar

野猪

deer

鹿

moose

麋鹿

dam

水坝

wind turbine

风力发电机

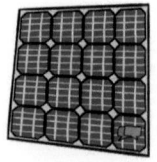

solar panel

太阳能电池板

climate

气候

restaurant

餐馆

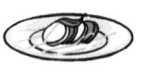

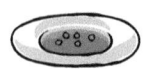

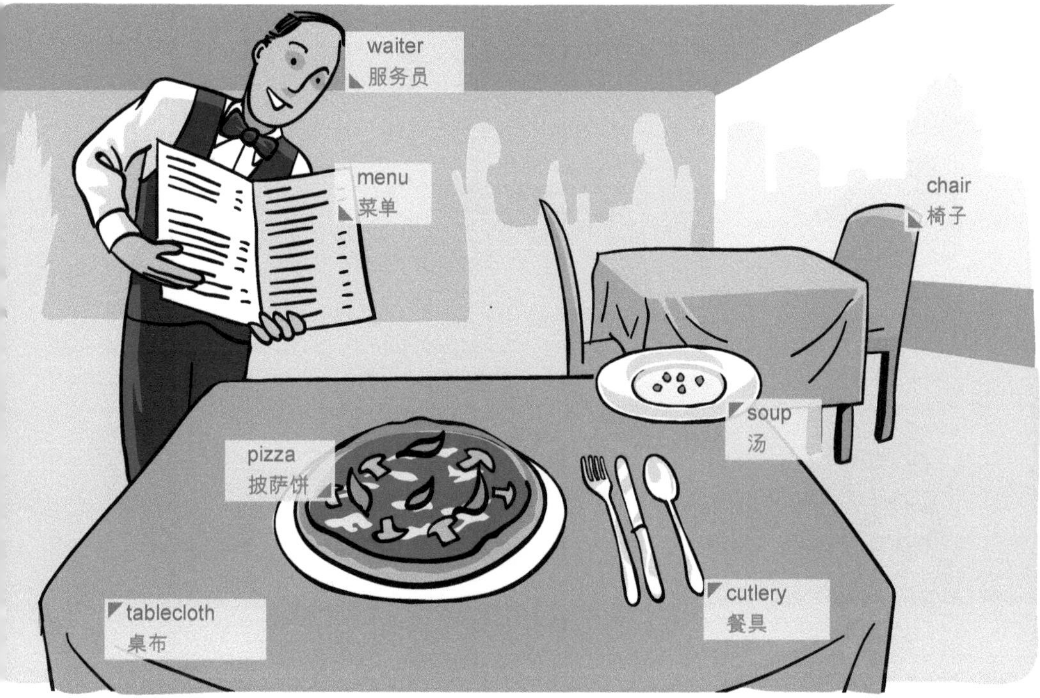
waiter
服务员
menu
菜单
chair
椅子
soup
汤
pizza
披萨饼
cutlery
餐具
tablecloth
桌布

starter

前菜

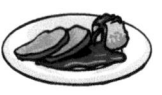

main course

主菜

dessert

甜点

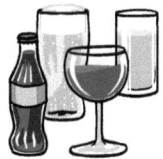

drinks

饮料

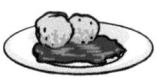

food

食物

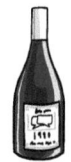

bottle

瓶子

fast food

快餐

street food

街边小吃

teapot

茶壶

sugar bowl

糖盒

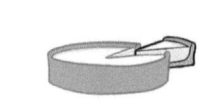

portion

一份饭菜

espresso machine

意式咖啡机

high chair

高脚椅

bill

账单

tray

托盘

knife

刀

fork

餐叉

spoon

勺子

teaspoon

茶匙

serviette

餐巾

glass

玻璃杯

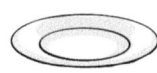

plate

碟子

soup plate

汤盘

saucer

碟子

sauce

酱

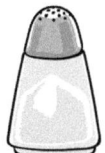

salt shaker

盐瓶

pepper mill

胡椒磨

vinegar

醋

oil

食用油

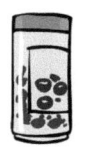

spices

调味料

ketchup

番茄酱

mustard

芥末

mayonnaise

蛋黄酱

supermarket
超市

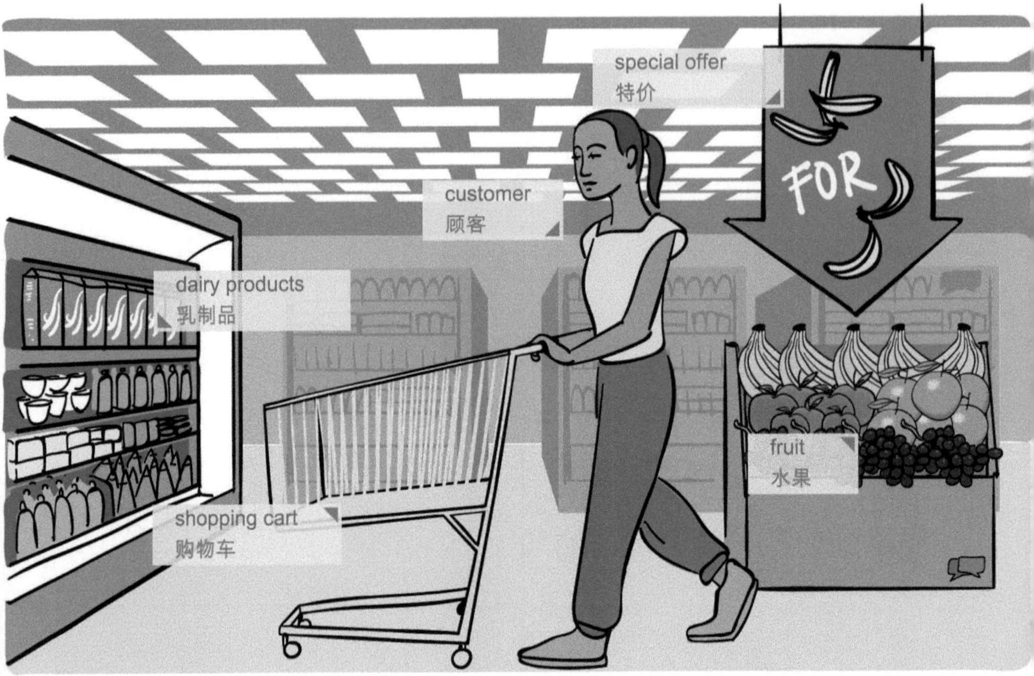

special offer
特价
FOR
customer
顾客
dairy products
乳制品
fruit
水果
shopping cart
购物车

BUTCHERS

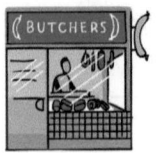

butcher's shop
肉铺

BAKERY

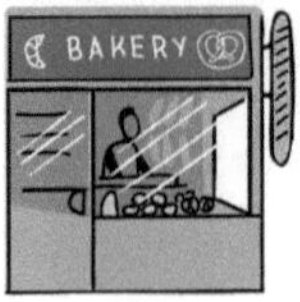

bakery
面包房

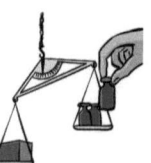

weigh
称重

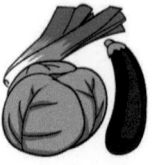

vegetables
蔬菜

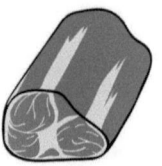

meat
肉

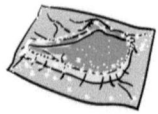

frozen food
冷冻食品

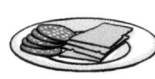

cold cuts

冷盘

canned food

罐头食品

detergent

洗衣粉

candy

甜食

household products

日用品

cleaning products

清洁用品

sales representative

销售员

cash register

收银机

cashier

收银员

shopping list

购物清单

opening hours

开放时间

wallet

钱包

credit card

信用卡

bag

袋子

plastic bag

塑料袋

drinks

饮料

water
水

juice
果汁

milk
牛奶

coke
可乐

wine
红酒

beer
啤酒

alcohol
酒

cocoa
可可

tea
茶

coffee
咖啡

espresso
意式浓缩咖啡

cappuccino
卡布奇诺

banana

香蕉

apple

苹果

orange

橙子

melon

西瓜

lemon

柠檬

carrot

胡萝卜

garlic

大蒜

bamboo

竹子

onion

洋葱

mushroom

蘑菇

nuts

坚果

noodles

面条

spaghetti

意大利面条

rice

米饭

salad

沙拉

fries

薯条

fried potatoes

炸土豆

pizza

披萨饼

hamburger

汉堡包

sandwich

三明治

escalope

炸猪排

ham

火腿

salami

萨拉米

sausage

香肠

chicken

鸡肉

roast

烤肉

fish

鱼

porridge oats

燕麦片

muesli

穆兹利

cornflakes

玉米片

flour

面粉

croissant

羊角面包

bread roll

面包卷

bread

面包

toast

烤面包

cookies

饼干

butter

黄油

curd

凝乳

cake

蛋糕

egg

蛋

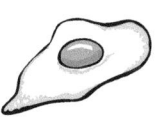

fried egg

煎蛋

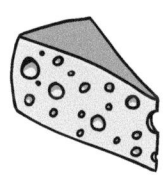

cheese

奶酪

ice cream

冰激凌

sugar

糖

honey

蜂蜜

jelly

果酱

nougat cream

巧克力酱

curry

咖喱饭

farm
农场

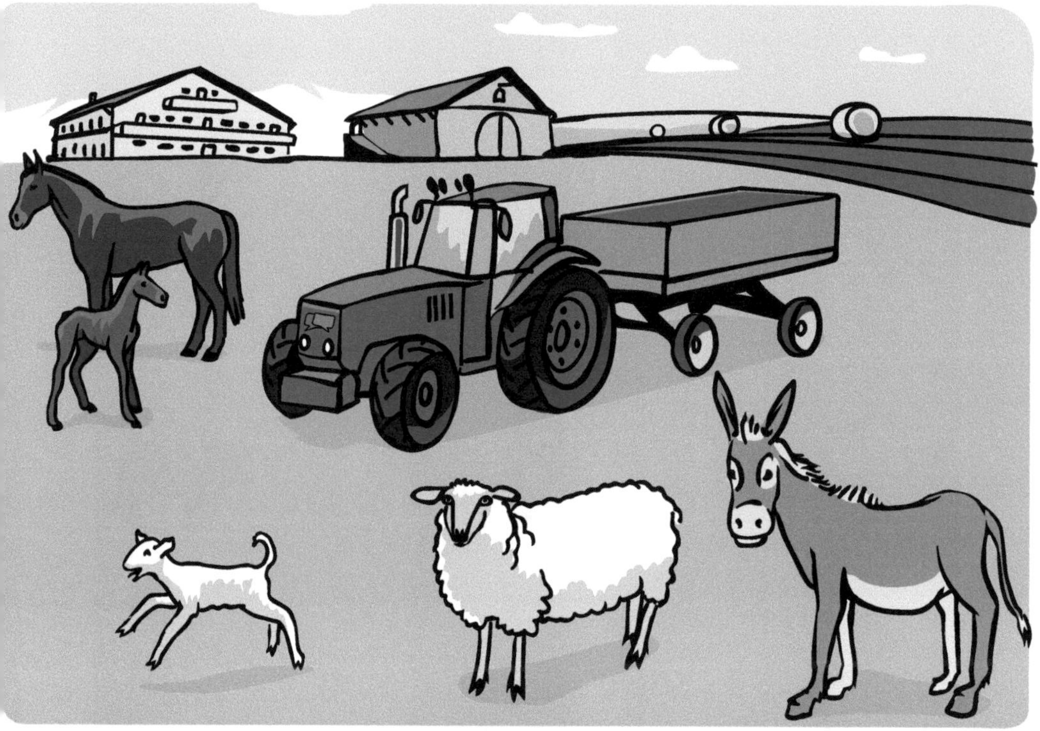

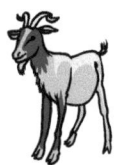

goat

山羊

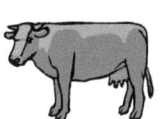

cow

奶牛

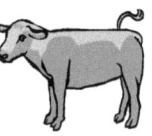

calf

牛犊

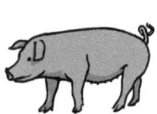

pig

猪

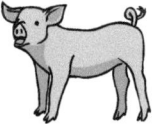

piglet

小猪

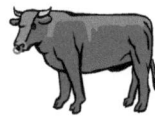

bull

公牛

goose

鹅

duck

鸭

chick

小鸡

hen

母鸡

cockerel

公鸡

rat

鼠

cat

猫

mouse

老鼠

ox

牛

dog

狗

dog house

狗屋

garden hose

花园浇水软管

watering can

洒水壶

scythe

长柄大镰刀

plow

犁

sickle

镰刀

hoe

锄头

pitchfork

长柄草耙

axe

斧头

pushcart

独轮手推车

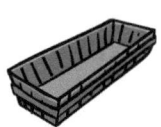

trough

饲料槽

milk can

牛奶罐

sack

麻布袋

fence

栅栏

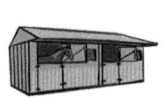

stable

马厩

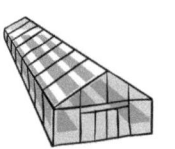

greenhouse

温室

soil

土壤

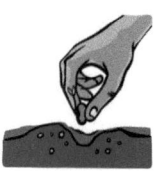

seed

种子

fertilizer

肥料

combine harvester

联合收割机

harvest

收割

harvest

收割

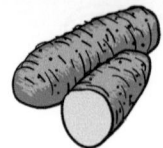

yams

山药

wheat

小麦

soya

大豆

potato

土豆

corn

玉米

rapeseed

油菜籽

fruit tree

果树

manioc

树薯

grain

谷物

house
房子

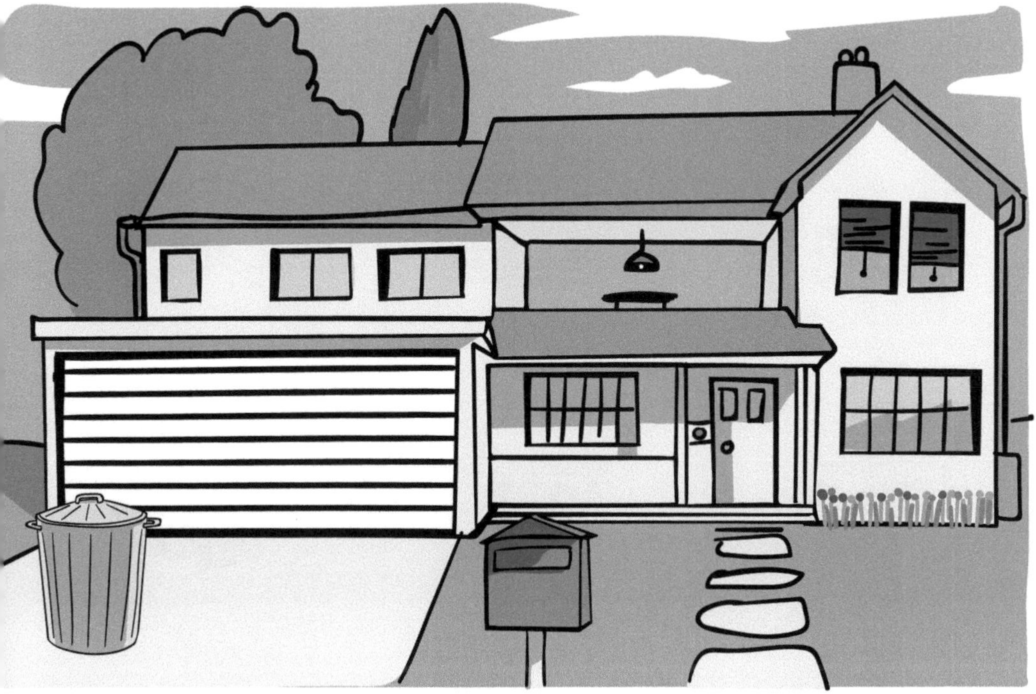

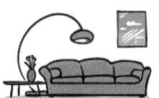

living room
客厅

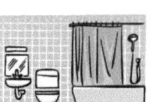

bathroom
浴室

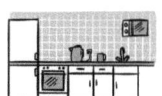

kitchen
厨房

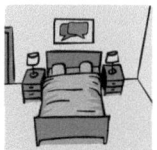

bedroom
卧室

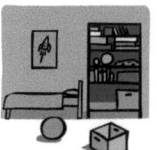

kids room
儿童房

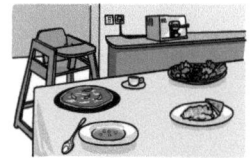

dining room
餐厅

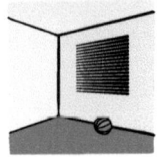

floor

地板

wall

墙壁

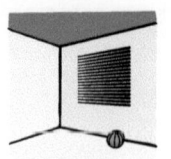

ceiling

吊顶

cellar

地窖

sauna

桑拿

balcony

阳台

terrace

露台

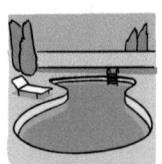

pool

游泳池

lawn mower

割草机

sheet

被单

bedspread

床罩

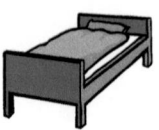

bed

床

broom

扫帚

bucket

水桶

switch

开关

living room

客厅

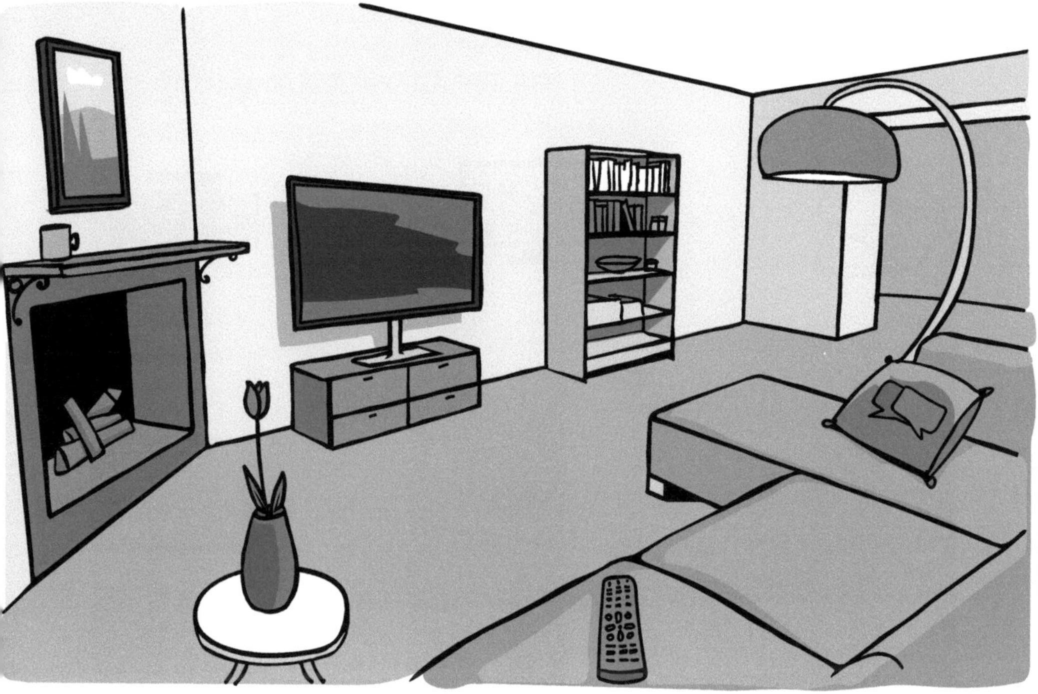

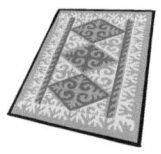

carpet

地毯

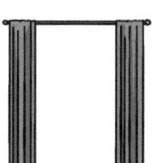

drape

窗帘

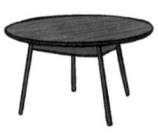

table

餐桌

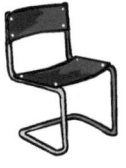

chair

椅子

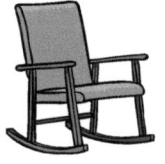

rocking chair

摇椅

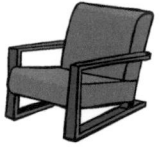

armchair

扶手椅

book

书

blanket

毯子

decoration

装饰品

firewood

木柴

film

电影

stereo system

高保真音响

key

钥匙

newspaper

报纸

painting

油画

poster

海报

radio

收音机

notebook

笔记本

vacuum cleaner

吸尘器

cactus

仙人掌

candle

蜡烛

kitchen
厨房

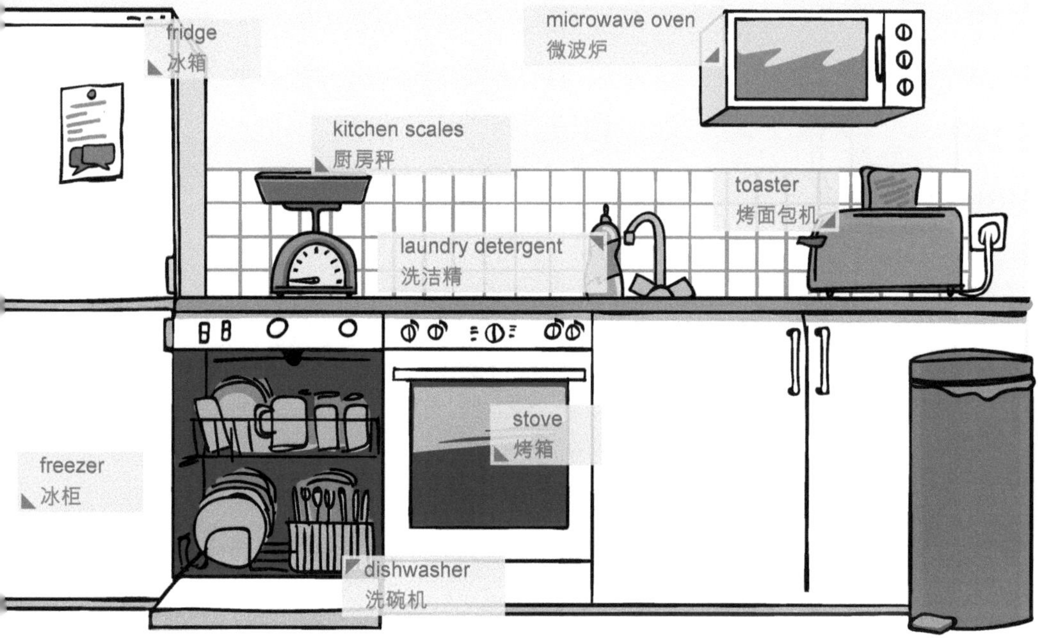
fridge
冰箱
microwave oven
微波炉
kitchen scales
厨房秤
toaster
烤面包机
laundry detergent
洗洁精
stove
烤箱
freezer
冰柜
dishwasher
洗碗机

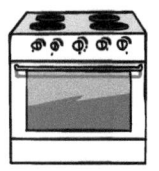

cooker
炊具

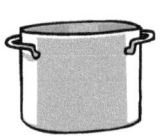

pot
锅

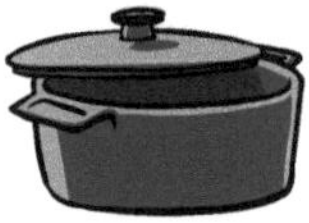

cast-iron pot
铸铁锅

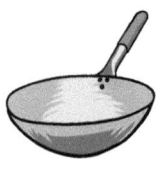

wok / kadai
炒锅

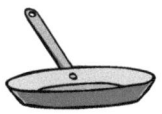

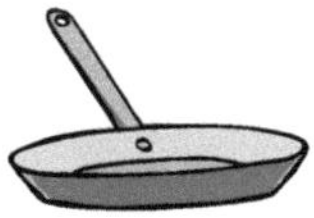
pan
平底锅

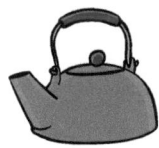

kettle
水壶

steamer

蒸锅

baking tray

烤盘

crockery

陶瓷锅

mug

马克杯

bowl

碗

chopsticks

筷子

ladle

长柄勺

spatula

铲子

whisk

搅拌器

strainer

滤网

sieve

筛子

grater

磨碎机

mortar

研钵

barbecue

烧烤

fireplace

明火

chopping board

菜板

rolling pin

擀面杖

corkscrew

开瓶器

can

罐子

can opener

开罐器

oven cloth

隔热手套

sink

水槽

brush

刷子

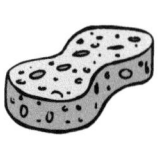

sponge

海绵

blender

搅拌机

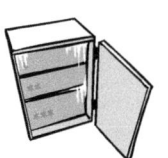

deep freezer

冷藏箱

baby bottle

奶瓶

tap

水龙头

bathroom

浴室

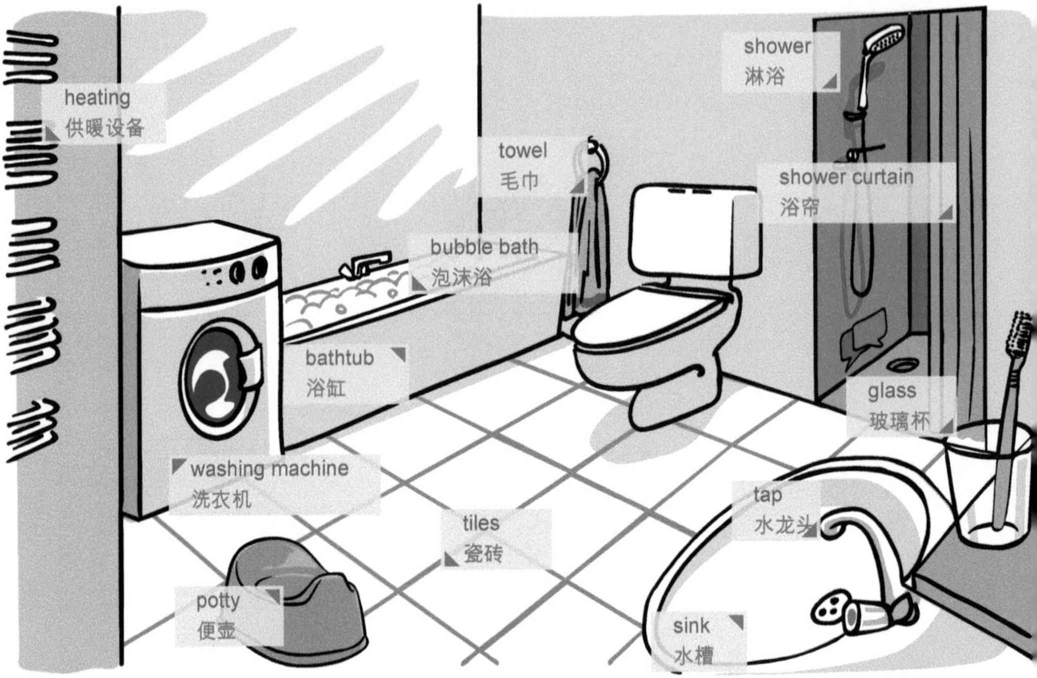

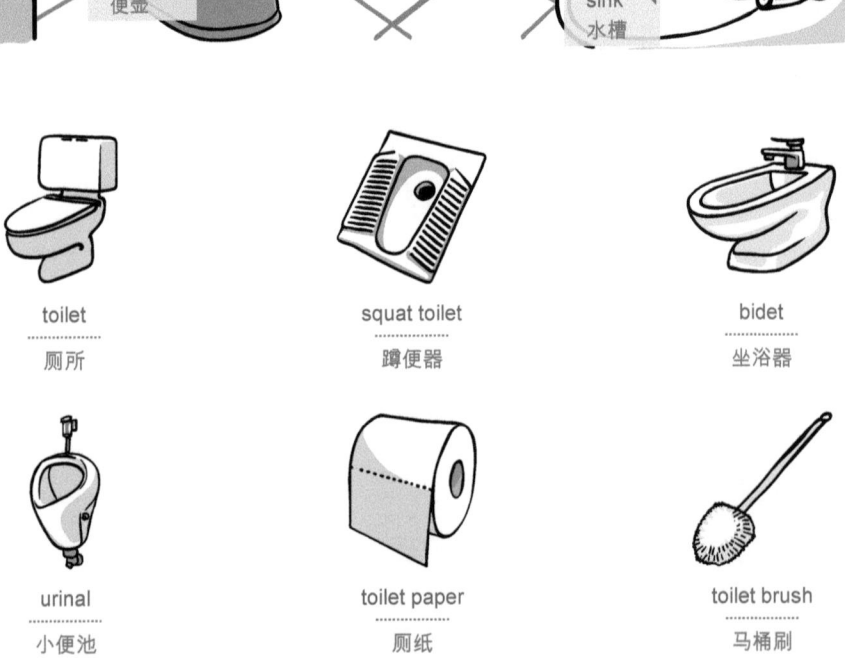

heating
供暖设备
towel
毛巾
shower
淋浴
shower curtain
浴帘
bubble bath
泡沫浴
bathtub
浴缸
glass
玻璃杯
washing machine
洗衣机
tap
水龙头
tiles
瓷砖
potty
便壶
sink
水槽

toilet

厕所

squat toilet

蹲便器

bidet

坐浴器

urinal

小便池

toilet paper

厕纸

toilet brush

马桶刷

toothbrush

牙刷

toothpaste

牙膏

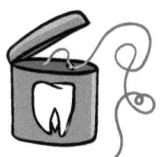

dental floss

牙线

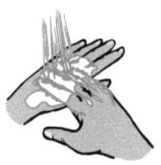

wash

洗

hand shower

手持式喷淋头

douche

冲洗器

basin

洗脸盆

back brush

擦背刷

soap

肥皂

shower gel

沐浴露

shampoo

洗发水

flannel

法兰绒

drain

排水

creme

乳霜

deodorant

除臭剂

mirror

镜子

hand mirror

手镜

razor

剃须刀

shaving foam

剃须泡沫

aftershave

须后水

comb

梳子

brush

刷子

hair-dryer

吹风机

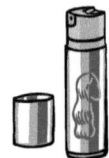

hairspray

喷发定型剂

makeup

化妆品

lipstick

唇膏

nail varnish

指甲油

cotton wool

化妆棉

nail scissors

指甲剪

perfume

香水

washbag

洗漱包

stool

凳子

weighing scales

计重秤

bathrobe

浴袍

rubber gloves

橡胶手套

tampon

卫生棉条

sanitary towel

卫生巾

chemical toilet

化学厕所

kids room
儿童房

alarm clock
闹钟
cuddly toy
毛绒玩具
toy car
玩具车
rattle
拨浪鼓
doll's house
玩具屋
present
礼物

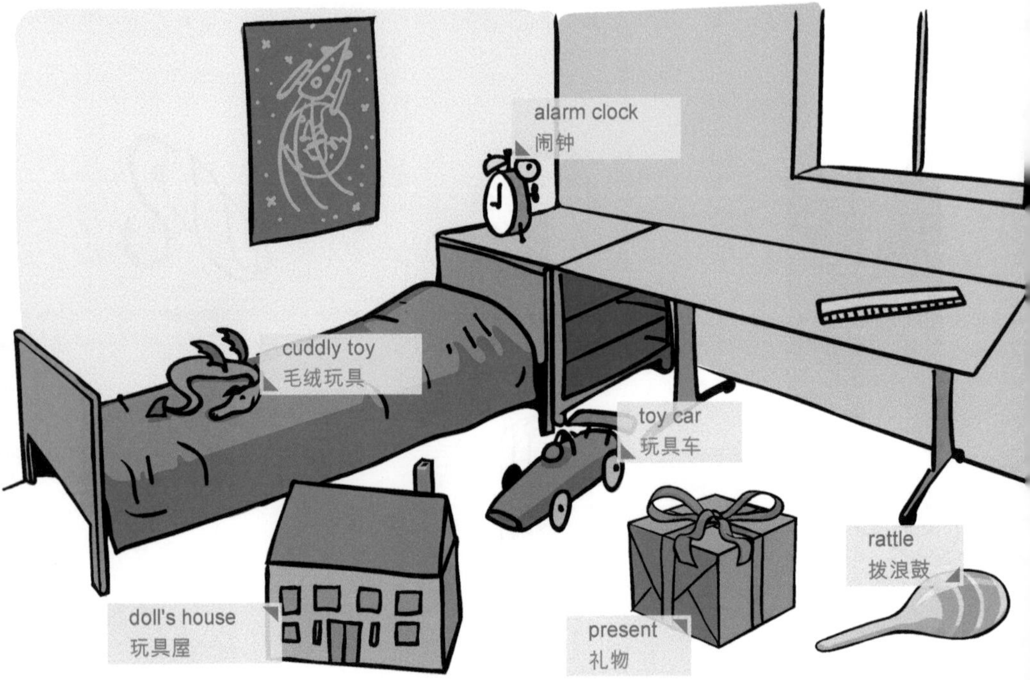

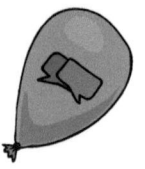

balloon

气球

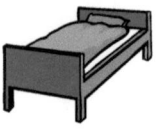

bed

床

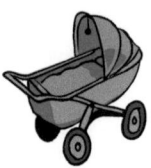

stroller

（洋娃娃用）婴儿车

deck of cards

扑克牌

jigsaw

拼图

SUPER
MEGA

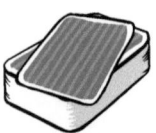

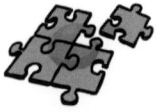

comic

漫画

lego bricks

乐高积木

toy blocks

积木玩具

action figure

玩具人

romper suit

婴儿服

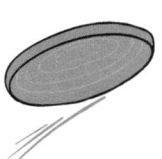

frisbee

飞盘

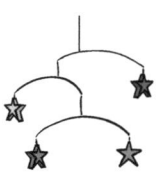

mobile

床铃玩具

board game

棋盘游戏

dice

骰子

model train set

火车模型

pacifier

安抚奶嘴

party

聚会

picture book

绘本

ball

球

doll

洋娃娃

play

玩

sandpit

沙坑

swing

秋千

toys

玩具

video game console

游戏机

tricycle

三轮车

teddy bear

泰迪熊

wardrobe

衣柜

clothing

衣服

socks

袜子

stockings

长袜

tights

紧身裤

scarf
围巾

umbrella
雨伞

belt
皮带

t-shirt
T恤

boots
靴子

slippers
拖鞋

sneakers
运动鞋

sandals

凉鞋

shoes

鞋

rubber boots

雨靴

underwear

内裤

bra

胸罩

undershirt

背心

clothing - 衣服

body

身体

pants

裤子

jeans

牛仔裤

skirt

短裙

blouse

女式衬衫

shirt

衬衫

pullover

套头衫

sweater

卫衣

blazer

西装夹克

jacket

夹克

coat

外套

raincoat

雨衣

costume

套装

dress

连衣裙

wedding dress

婚纱

suit

西装

nightgown

睡袍

pajamas

睡衣

sari

莎丽

headscarf

头巾

turban

包头巾

burka

波卡

kaftan

卡夫坦

abaya

(阿拉伯式)长袍长袍

swimsuit

泳衣

trunks

男式泳裤

shorts

短裤

tracksuit

运动服

apron

围裙

gloves

手套

button

纽扣

glasses

眼镜

bracelet

手链

necklace

项链

ring

戒指

earring

耳环

cap

便帽

coat hanger

衣架

hat

帽子

tie

领带

zip

拉链

helmet

头盔

braces

背带

school uniform

校服

uniform

制服

clothing - 衣服

bib
围兜

pacifier
安抚奶嘴

diaper
尿不湿

office

办公室

server
服务器

filing cabinet
文件柜

printer
打印机

paper
纸

monitor
显示屏

mouse
鼠标

desk
办公桌

folder
文件夹

keyboard
键盘

waste-paper basket
废纸篓

chair
椅子

computer
电脑

coffee mug
咖啡杯

calculator
计算器

internet
因特网

office - 办公室

laptop

笔记本电脑

letter

信件

message

消息

cell phone

手机

network

网络

photocopier

复印机

software

软件

telephone

电话

plug socket

插座

fax machine

传真机

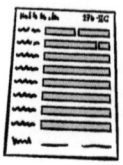

form

表格

document

文件

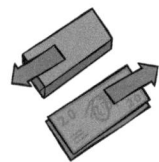

buy

买

pay

付钱

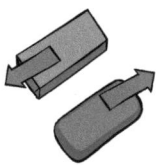

trade

交易

money

现金

dollar

美元

euro

欧元

yen

日元

rouble

卢布

Swiss franc

瑞士法郎

renminbi yuan

人民币

rupee

卢比

cash point

提款处

currency exchange office

外币兑换处

gold

金

silver

银

oil

石油

energy

能源

price

价格

contract

合同

tax

税金

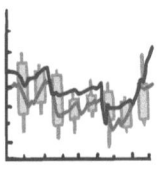

stock

股票

work

工作

employee

职员

employer

老板

factory

工厂

shop

商店

economy - 经济

police officer
警官

fireman
消防員

pilot
飛行員

doctor
医生

cook
厨師

gardener

園丁

carpenter

木匠

seamstress

裁縫

judge

法官

chemist

化学家

actor

演員

bus driver

公交车司机

taxi driver

出租车司机

fisherman

渔夫

cleaning lady

清洁女工

roofer

屋顶工

waiter

服务员

hunter

猎人

painter

画家

baker

面包师

electrician

电工

builder

建筑工人

engineer

工程师

butcher

屠夫

plumber

水管工

postman

邮递员

soldier

士兵

architect

建筑师

cashier

收银员

florist

花农

hairdresser

理发师

conductor

售票员

mechanic

机械师

captain

船长

dentist

牙医

scientist

科学家

rabbi

拉比

imam

伊玛目

monk

和尚

pastor

牧师

tools

工具

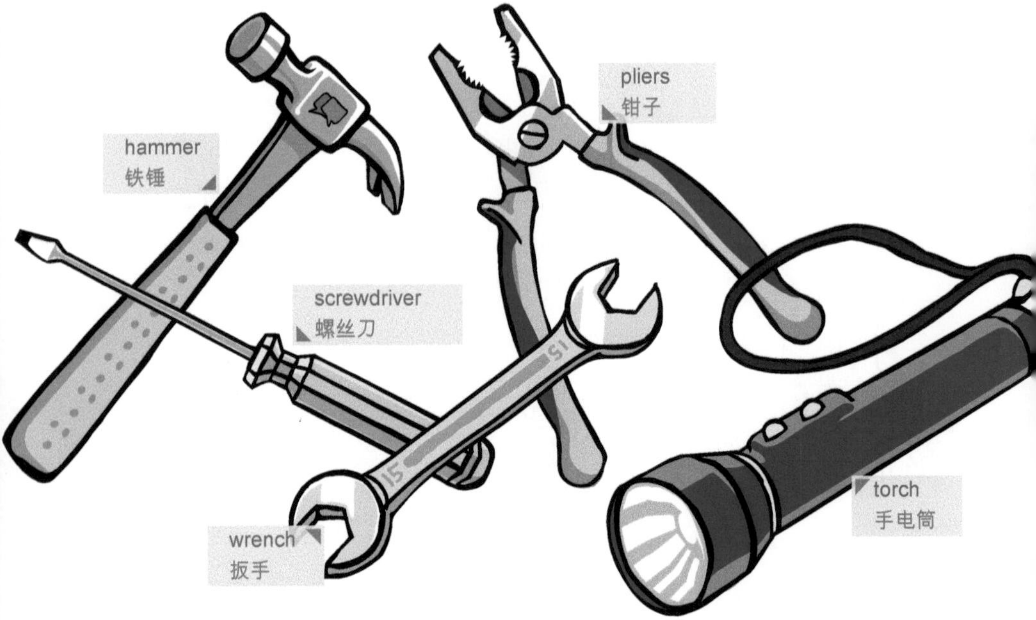

pliers
钳子
hammer
铁锤
screwdriver
螺丝刀
torch
手电筒
wrench
扳手

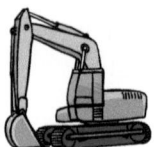

excavator

挖掘机

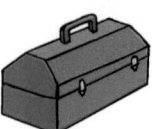

toolbox

工具箱

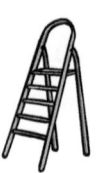

ladder

梯子

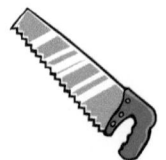

saw

锯子

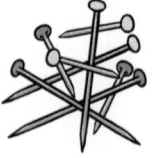

nails

钉子

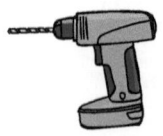

drill

钻机

repair

修

shovel

铲子

Damn!

靠！

dustpan

簸箕

paint can

油漆桶

screws

螺丝

musical instruments

乐器

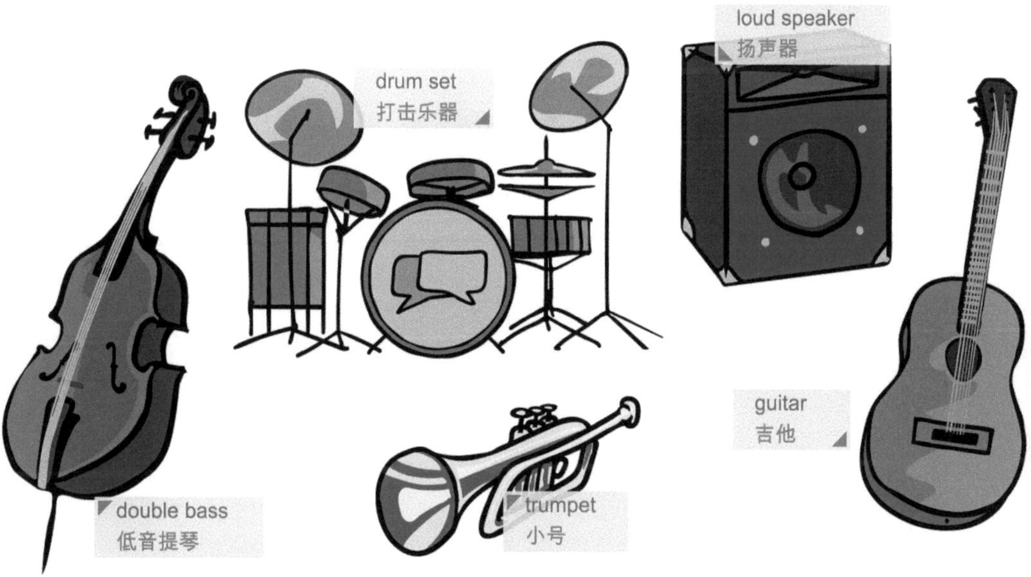

loud speaker
扬声器

drum set
打击乐器

guitar
吉他

double bass
低音提琴

trumpet
小号

piano

钢琴

violin

小提琴

bass

贝斯

timpani

定音鼓

drums

鼓

keyboard

电子琴

saxophone

萨克斯管

flute

长笛

microphone

麦克风

tiger
老虎

entrance
入口

cage
笼子

zebra
斑马

animal feed
动物饲料

panda
熊猫

animals

动物

elephant

大象

kangaroo

袋鼠

rhino

犀牛

gorilla

大猩猩

bear

熊

camel

骆驼

ostrich

鸵鸟

lion

狮子

monkey

猴子

flamingo

火烈鸟

parrot

鹦鹉

polar bear

北极熊

penguin

企鹅

shark

鲨鱼

peacock

孔雀

snake

蛇

crocodile

鳄鱼

zookeeper

动物园管理员

seal

海豹

jaguar

美洲豹

pony

矮种马

leopard

豹

hippo

河马

giraffe

长颈鹿

eagle

老鹰

boar

野猪

fish

鱼

turtle

龟

walrus

海象

fox

狐狸

gazelle

羚羊

American football
橄榄球

cycling
骑自行车

tennis
网球

basketball
篮球

swimming
游泳

boxing
拳击

ice hockey
冰球

soccer
英式足球

badminton
羽毛球

athletics
田径

handball
手球

skiing
滑雪

polo
马球

jump
跳

laugh
笑

hug
拥抱

walk
走路

sing
唱

dream
做梦

pray
祈祷

kiss
亲吻

write 书写	draw 画	show 展示
push 推	give 给	take 拿

have

有

do

做

be

当

stand

站

run

跑

pull

拉

throw

扔

fall

摔倒

lie

躺

wait

等待

carry

携带

sit

坐

get dressed

穿衣

sleep

睡觉

wake up

醒来

look at
看

cry
哭

stroke
抚摸

comb
梳头

talk
交谈

understand
明白

ask
问

listen
听

drink
喝

eat
吃

tidy up
清理

love
爱

cook
做饭

drive
开车

fly
飞

sail

航行

calculate

计算

read

读

learn

学习

work

工作

marry

结婚

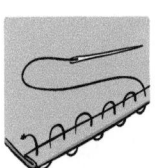

sew

缝

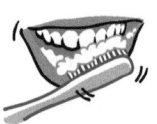

brush teeth

刷牙

kill

杀

smoke

抽烟

send

寄

grandmother
祖母

grandfather
祖父

father
父亲

mother
母亲

baby
婴童

daughter
女儿

son
儿子

guest
客人

aunt
阿姨

uncle
叔叔

brother
兄弟

sister
姐妹

body
身体

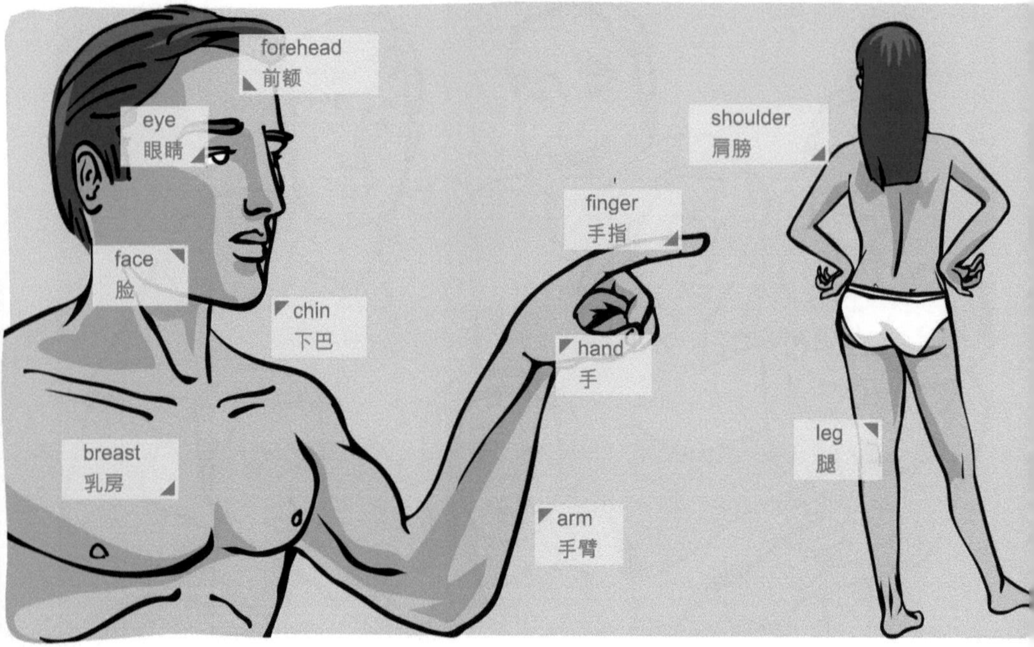

forehead
前额

eye
眼睛

shoulder
肩膀

finger
手指

face
脸

chin
下巴

hand
手

breast
乳房

leg
腿

arm
手臂

baby

婴童

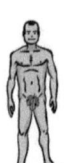

man

男人

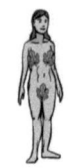

woman

女人

girl

女孩

boy

男孩

head

头

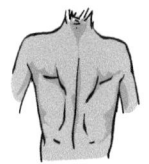

back

背部

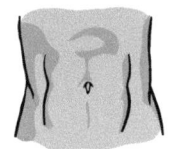

belly

肚子

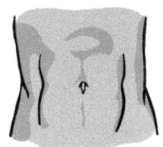

navel

肚脐

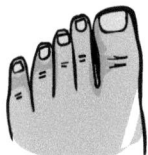

toe

脚趾

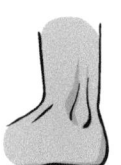

heel

脚后跟

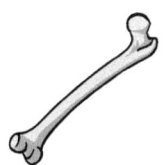

bone

骨头

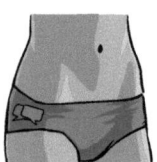

hip

臀部

knee

膝盖

elbow

手肘

nose

鼻子

buttocks

屁股

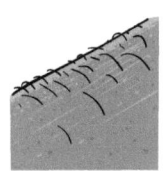

skin

皮肤

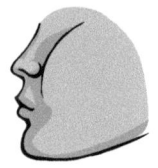

cheek

脸颊

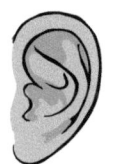

ear

耳朵

lip

嘴唇

mouth

嘴

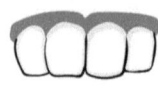

tooth

牙齿

tongue

舌头

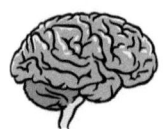

brain

脑

heart

心脏

muscle

肌肉

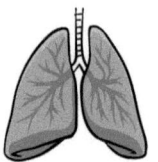

lung

肺

liver

肝脏

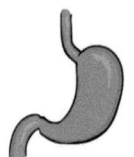

stomach

胃

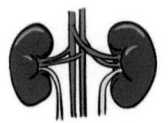

kidneys

肾脏

sex

性交

condom

避孕套

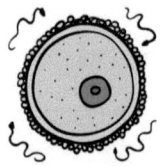

ovum

卵子

semen

精子

pregnancy

怀孕

body - 身体

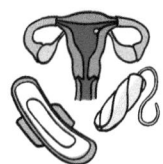

menstruation

月经

vagina

阴道

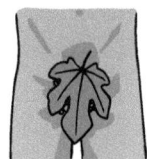

penis

阴茎

eyebrow

眉毛

hair

头发

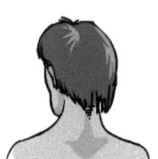

neck

脖子

hospital
医院

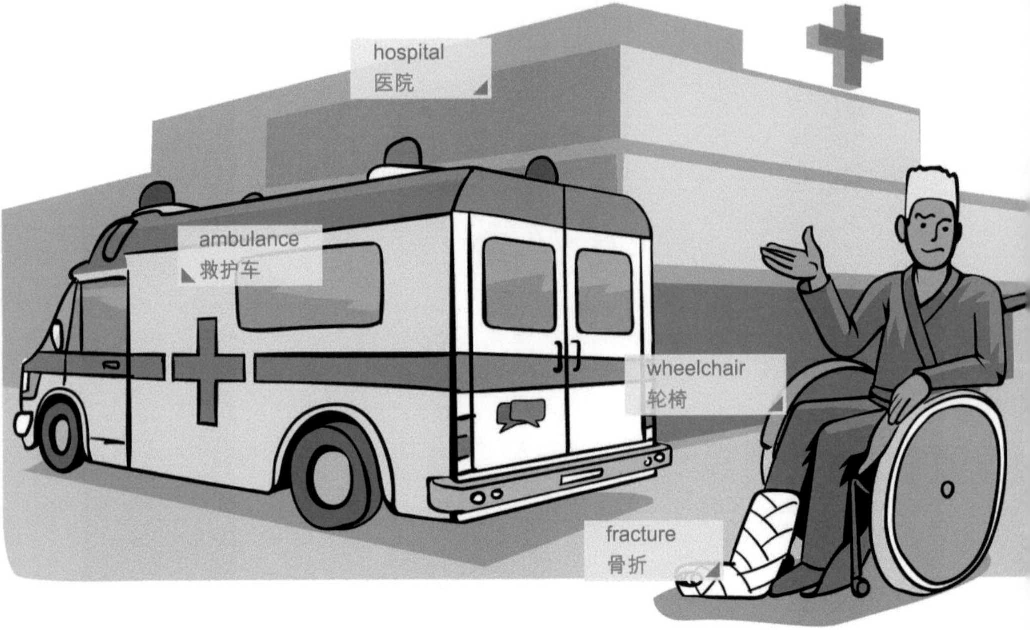

hospital
医院

ambulance
救护车

wheelchair
轮椅

fracture
骨折

doctor

医生

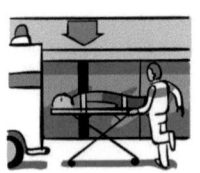

emergency room

急诊室

nurse

护士

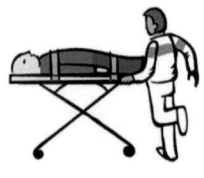

emergency

紧急情况

unconscious

昏迷

pain

痛

injury

受伤

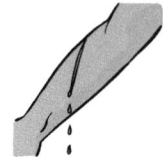

bleeding

出血

heart attack

心脏病发作

stroke

中风

allergy

过敏

cough

咳嗽

fever

发烧

flu

流感

diarrhea

腹泻

headache

头痛

cancer

癌症

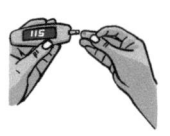

diabetes

糖尿病

surgeon

外科医生

scalpel

手术刀

operation

手术

hospital - 医院

CT

CT

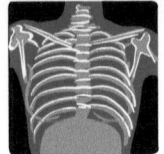

x-ray

X光

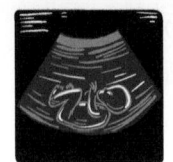

ultrasound

超声波

face mask

口罩

disease

疾病

waiting room

候诊室

crutch

拐杖

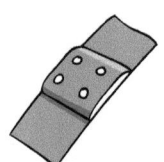

plaster

石膏

bandage

绷带

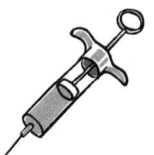

injection

注射

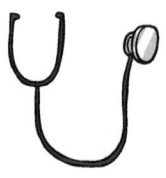

stethoscope

听诊器

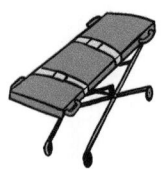

stretcher

担架

clinical thermometer

体温计

birth

出生

overweight

超重

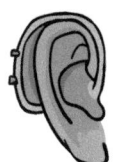

hearing aid

助听器

disinfectant

消毒液

infection

感染

virus

病毒

HIV / AIDS

艾滋病

medicine

药物

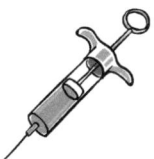

vaccination

接种疫苗

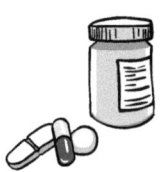

tablets

药片

pill

药丸

emergency call

急救电话

blood pressure monitor

血压计

ill / healthy

生病/健康

Help!
救命！

alarm
警报

assault
突击

attack
攻击

danger
危险

emergency exit
紧急出口

Fire!
着火啦！

fire extinguisher
灭火器

accident
意外

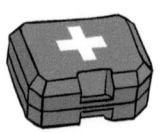

first-aid kit
急救箱

SOS
呼救信号

police
警察

Europe

欧洲

North America

北美洲

South America

南美洲

Africa

非洲

Asia

亚洲

Australia

澳洲

Atlantic

大西洋

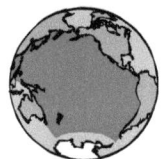

Pacific

太平洋

Indian Ocean

印度洋

Antarctic Ocean

南冰洋

Arctic Ocean

北冰洋

North pole

北极

South pole

南极

Antarctica

南极洲

earth

地球

land

陆地

sea

海

island

岛

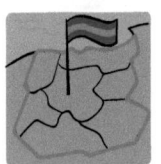

nation

国家

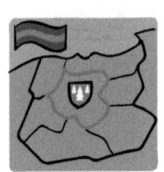

state

国家

clock face

钟面

hour hand

时针

minute hand

分针

second hand

秒针

What time is it?

现在几点？

day

天

time

时间

now

现在

digital watch

电子表

minute

分

hour

时

week

周

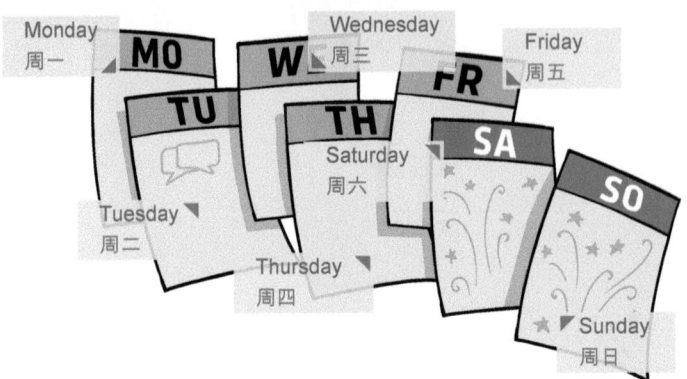

Monday
周一

MO

Tuesday
周二

TU

Wednesday
周三

W

Thursday
周四

TH

Friday
周五

FR

Saturday
周六

SA

Sunday
周日

SO

yesterday

昨天

today

今天

tomorrow

明天

morning

早晨

noon

中午

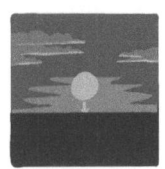

evening

晚上

MO	TU	WE	TH	FR	SA	SU
1	2	3	4	5	6	7
8	9	10	11	12	13	14
15	16	17	18	19	20	21
22	23	24	25	26	27	28
29	30	31	1	2	3	4

workdays

工作日

MO	TU	WE	TH	FR	SA	SU
1	2	3	4	5	6	7
8	9	10	11	12	13	14
15	16	17	18	19	20	21
22	23	24	25	26	27	28
29	30	31	1	2	3	4

weekend

周末

year
年

rain
雨
spring
春
summer
夏
wind
风
fall
秋
snow
雪
winter
冬

4.APRIL 11°
5.APRIL 4°
6.APRIL 13°
7.APRIL 8°
8.APRIL 10°

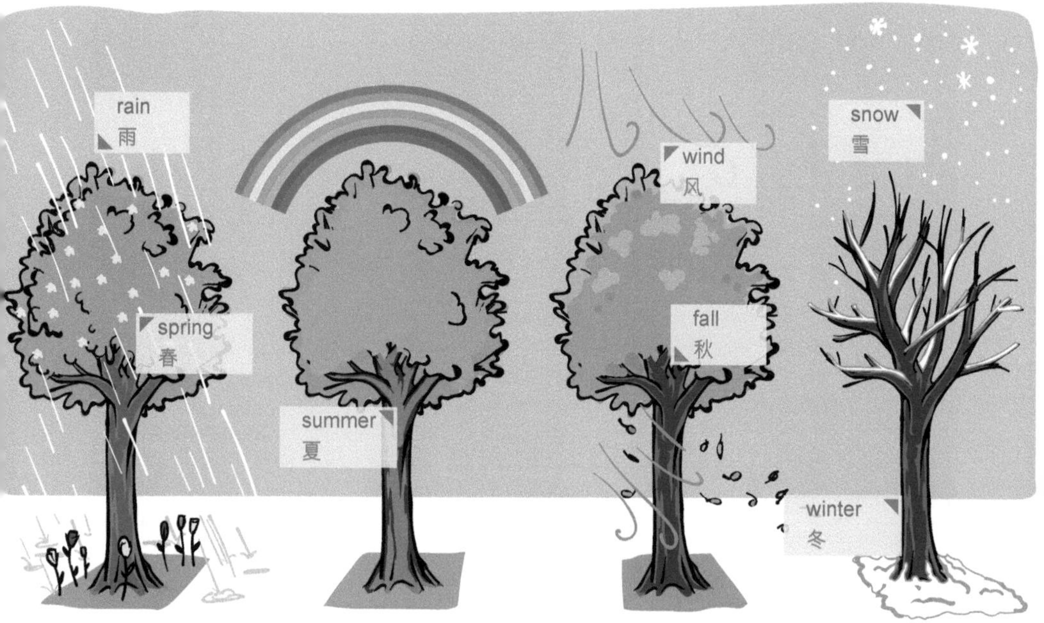

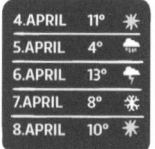

weather forecast

天气预报

F
C
120
90
60
30
0
-30
40
30
20
10
0
-10
-20

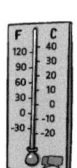

thermometer

温度计

sunshine

阳光

cloud

云

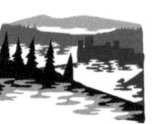

fog

雾

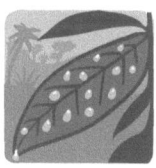

humidity

潮湿

lightning

闪电

thunder

打雷

storm

风暴

hail

冰雹

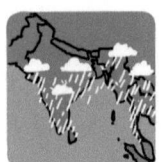

monsoon

季风

flood

洪水

ice

冰

January

一月

February

二月

March

三月

April

四月

May

五月

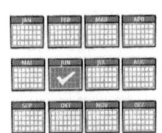

June

六月

July

七月

August

八月

year - 年

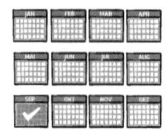

September

九月

October

十月

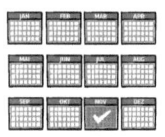

November

十一月

December

十二月

shapes

形状

circle

圆形

square

正方形

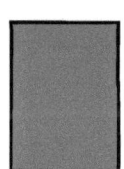

rectangle

长方形

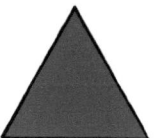

triangle

三角形

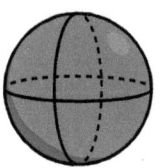

sphere

球体

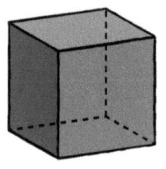

cube

立方体

white

白

yellow

黄

orange

橙

pink

粉

red

红

purple

紫

blue

蓝

green

绿

brown

棕

gray

灰

black

黑

a lot / a little

很多/少许

angry / calm

生气/平静

beautiful / ugly

美/丑

beginning / end

首/尾

big / small

大/小

bright / dark

明/暗

brother / sister

兄弟/姐妹

clean / dirty

干净/肮脏

complete / incomplete

完整/缺失

day / night

白天/晚上

dead / alive

死/生

wide / narrow

宽/窄

edible / inedible

可食用/非食用

evil / kind

邪恶/善良

excited / bored

兴奋/无聊

fat / thin

胖/瘦

first / last

第一/最后

friend / enemy

朋友/敌人

full / empty

满/空

hard / soft

硬/软

heavy / light

重/轻

hunger / thirst

饿/渴

ill / healthy

生病/健康

illegal / legal

非法/合法

intelligent / stupid

聪明/愚笨

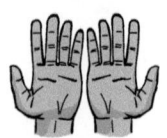

left / right

左/右

near / far

近/远

new / used

新/旧

nothing / something

没有/有些

old / young

老/幼

on / off

开/关

open / closed

打开/合上

quiet / loud

安静/吵闹

rich / poor

富/穷

right / wrong

对/错

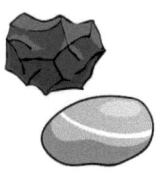

rough / smooth

粗糙/光滑

sad / happy

伤心/高兴

short / long

短/长

slow / fast

慢/快

wet / dry

湿/干

warm / cool

温暖/凉爽

war / peace

战争/和平

opposites - 反义词

0

zero

零

1

one

一

2

two

二

3

three

三

4

four

四

5

five

五

6

six

六

7

seven

七

8

eight

八

9

nine

九

10

ten

十

11

eleven

十一

12

twelve

十二

13

thirteen

十三

14

fourteen

十四

15

fifteen

十五

16

sixteen

十六

17

seventeen

十七

18

eighteen

十八

19

nineteen

十九

20

twenty

二十

100

hundred

百

1.000

thousand

千

1.000.000

million

百万

English
英语

American English
美式英语

Chinese Mandarin
普通话

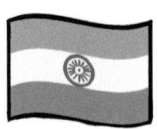

Hindi
印地语

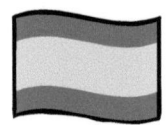

Spanish
西班牙语

French
法语

Arabic
阿拉伯语

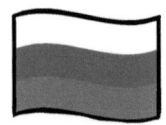

Russian
俄语

Portuguese
葡萄牙语

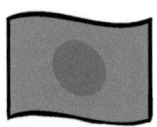

Bengali
孟加拉语

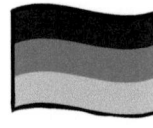

German
德语

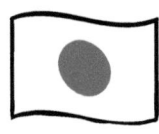

Japanese
日语

I

我

you

你

he / she / it

他/她/它

we

我们

you

你们

they

他们

who?

谁？

what?

什么？

how?

怎样？

where?

哪里？

when?

什么时候？

name

名字

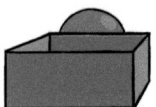

behind

后面

in

里面

in front of

前面

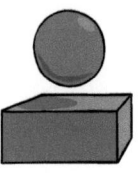

over

上方

on

上面

under

下面

beside

旁边

between

中间

place

地点